ICONIC DESIGNS

GREAT
AIRCRAFT
DESIGNS

1900–TODAY

Richard Spilsbury

heinemann
raintree

Edited by Clare Lewis and Abby Colich
Designed by Richard Parker
Original illustrations © Capstone Global Library Ltd. 2015
Illustrated by HL Studios
Picture research by Jo Miller
Production by Victoria Fitzgerald
Originated by Capstone Global Library Ltd.
Printed and bound in China by Leo Paper Products

19 18 17 16 15
10 9 8 7 6 5 4 3 2 1

Library of Congress Cataloging-in-Publication Data

Spilsbury, Richard, 1963-
  Great aircraft designs 1900-today / Richard Spilsbury.
    pages cm.—(Iconic designs)
  Includes bibliographical references and index.
  ISBN 978-1-4846-2616-0 (hb)—ISBN 978-1-4846-2621-4 (pb)—ISBN 978-1-4846-2631-3 (ebook) 1.
Airplanes—History—Juvenile literature. I. Title. II. Title: Great aircraft designs nineteen hundred-today.
  TL547.S71784 2015
  629.13—dc23   2015000274

Acknowledgments
We would like to thank the following for permission to reproduce photographs: Alamy: Radius Images, 35, ZUMA Press Inc., 21; Corbis: Bettmann, 12, 19, 23, Transtock, 31; Corel, 4; Getty Images, 9, AFP/AFP, 13, SSPL, 18, Stephen Brashear, 34, Underwood Archives, 15; NASA, 38, 39, Carla Thomas, 42; Newscom: Everett Collection, 6, 14, KRT/Chuck Kennedy, 8, Mirrorpix/Official, 10, Robert Harding/Ian Griffiths, 36, UIG Universal Images Group/ Mondadori Collection, 20; Science Source, 28; Shutterstock: Kletr, 11, Lars Christensen, 32, Melissa Madia, 5, Paul Drabot, cover (inset), 16, 25; SuperStock, 33, Transtock, 30; The Image Works: Roger-Viollet, 17; U.S. Air Force photo by Staff Sgt. Bennie J. Davis III, 40, Staff Sgt. Tiffany Trojca, 43; Wikimedia: Department of Defense/PFC E. E. Green, U.S. Army, 24, LA (PHOT) Billy Bunting, cover, 6, Stahlkocher, 41

Design Elements
Shutterstock: franco's photos, Jason Winter, URRRA

CONTENTS

Some words are shown in bold, **like this**. You can find out what they mean by looking in the glossary.

INTRODUCING ICONIC AIRCRAFT

Aircraft come in many amazing designs, from giant jumbo jets and sleek stealth bombers to helicopters and **airships**. Every different type of aircraft is the product of a designer or team of designers.

Flight design

There is a lot involved in aircraft design. Designers have to use materials that make aircraft light but strong. They have to consider shape, size, safety, cost, and what the aircraft will be used for. Aircraft may have to be comfortable for passengers or roomy enough to carry cargo. Aircraft are very expensive and safety is essential, so **engineers** build models of a new aircraft to test how it will fly before building the real thing.

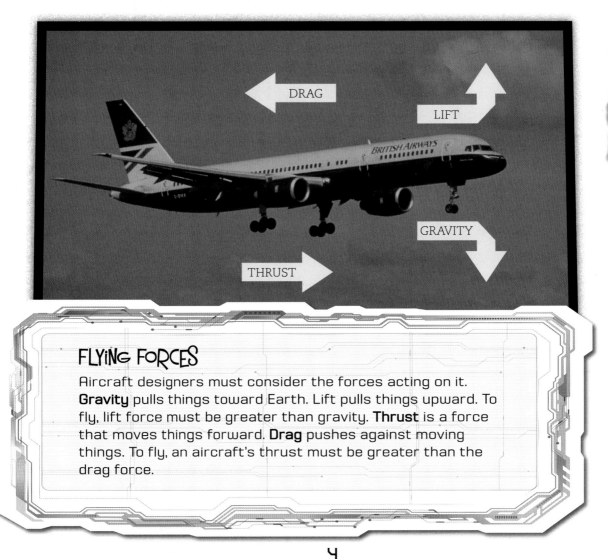

FLYING FORCES

Aircraft designers must consider the forces acting on it. **Gravity** pulls things toward Earth. Lift pulls things upward. To fly, lift force must be greater than gravity. **Thrust** is a force that moves things forward. **Drag** pushes against moving things. To fly, an aircraft's thrust must be greater than the drag force.

First flight

The first successful aircraft was built by France's Montgolfier brothers in 1783. The brothers knew that hot air rises, so they realized that filling a giant paper and silk balloon with hot air could carry a basket into the sky. The first passengers on this hot-air balloon were a duck, a chicken, and a sheep! The hot-air balloon is one iconic design of aircraft. In this book, we are going to look at many others.

Today's hot-air balloons work in the same way as the first one. However, they now use modern materials to create some amazing shapes and designs that can travel long and far.

WHAT IS AN ICONIC AIRCRAFT?

Iconic aircraft are the most famous aircraft. Some are famous because they did something new or did it better than other aircraft. Some were used by many people. Some are famous because they were beautifully designed.

Wright Flyer

FAST FACTS

Date: 1903
Designer: Orville and Wilbur Wright
Wingspan: 40.3 feet (12.2 meters)
Special features: **biplane**, single engine, 2 **propellers** at rear
Did you know? The engine was positioned right of center, to balance the weight of the pilot on the left.

Throughout the 19th century, people had experimented with flying like birds. Experiments using flapping wings failed, but some people developed **gliders** that could soar for hundreds of feet. However, none could achieve sustained, continuous flight until two brothers, Orville and Wilbur Wright, invented the Wright Flyer.

Wilbur and Orville Wright were aircraft pioneers. Their designs were based on lots of observation and testing.

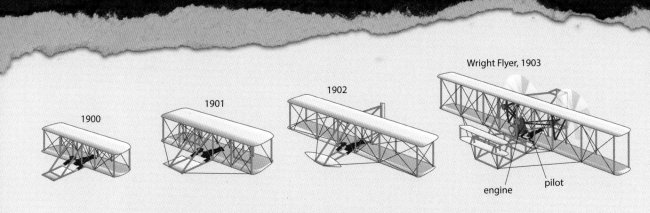

1900　1901　1902　Wright Flyer, 1903

engine　pilot

Between 1900 and 1902, the Wright brothers built and tested several glider prototypes. They used bigger and bigger wings. The Flyer was the biggest of all to carry the weight of a pilot and an engine.

Wing shapes

The Wright brothers already knew from what they had read about gliders that their aircraft should have wings with a curved top, called **airfoils**. These produce lift while the glider is going forward. How? Air moving over the curved top flows faster, so it pushes less on the wing than the air flowing below the wing. They used two wings for greater lift than one wing, using a framework of light wood covered with tightly stretched canvas.

WORLD OF DESIGN

Prototype

A prototype is a model or trial design that can be tested for how well it works before building the actual object.

Taking control

The Wright brothers observed how birds angled their wings and feathers to dive or fly upward and roll left and right. They then used these observations to control their aircraft. They added a flap, or elevator, to the front that could be angled using wires to go up or down. Pulling on other wires twisted the wing tips to make the aircraft turn left or right.

Testing, testing

The Wright brothers tested different sizes and shapes of wing, elevators, and other parts to develop a working aircraft. They did this by flying **prototypes** in a special room with a large fan to blow air, known as a **wind tunnel**.

Power

The Wright brothers knew they needed a motor for continuous flight. So they created a gasoline engine that was much lighter than existing car engines. Using a chain, they linked a spinning wheel on the engine to two light metal, airfoil-shaped propellers. These pushed air backward to produce horizontal thrust.

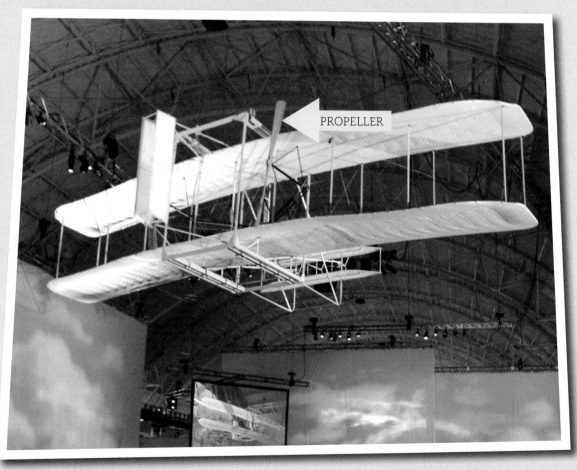

PROPELLER

You can see one of the long, thin propellers on this replica of the original Wright Flyer.

First flight

The Wright *Flyer I* first successfully took off using its own power and flew for 12 seconds in 1903 in the United States. The pilot, Orville, lay on the lower wing. He pulled cables to control *Flyer I* by hand and by shifting his hips. On later flights, the aircraft went farther but was destroyed when it was blown over in the wind. The Wrights built a copy. But the *Flyer II* proved to have only enough power for short flights.

The Wright Flyer takes a test flight in 1904, with representatives of the U.S. Army looking on. It was already clear that the invention could help soldiers.

Successful aircraft

In 1905, the Wrights came up with a bigger, more powerful aircraft. On October 5, Wilbur flew the *Flyer III* for 39 minutes, covering over 24 miles (38 kilometers) and flying figure-eight turns! It was the world's first practical aircraft, and the Wrights set up a factory to keep up with demand. They also trained pilots. In 1909, the U.S. Army started to buy Flyers. By 1911, military Flyers were being used for dropping bombs, observing the enemy from the air, and parachute jumps.

SOPWITH CAMEL

FAST FACTS

Type of aircraft: Fighter plane
Produced by: Sopwith Aviation Company
First flown in: 1916

Like the Wright Flyer, the Sopwith Camel was a biplane. It was also the most famous British fighter plane of World War I (1914–1918). It shot down more enemy aircraft than any other plane. The Camel got its name from the hump-shaped metal cover that went over the two machine guns mounted in front of the pilot. These guns pointed through the propeller to fire at whatever was directly in front of the plane. A special system ensured that the guns could only fire when the propellers were out of the way.

The Sopwith Camel was 18 feet, 9 inches (5.7 meters) long and had a wingspan of 28 feet (8.5 meters).

Power plane

The Sopwith Camel looked like a normal biplane. The **fuselage** was a wooden, box-like structure. It was covered with aluminum at the front, plywood around the **cockpit**, and fabric over the back and tail. However, the designers wanted the Camel to be able to turn very quickly in an air fight, so they put the engine, fuel tank, cockpit, and guns close together in the front third of the plane. This helped the plane to turn quickly. If not handled carefully, though, the plane could easily go into a spin and crash. In fact, almost as many Camel pilots were killed in accidents as were killed by the enemy.

GERMAN RiVAL

German flying ace Baron von Richthofen was famous for winning aircraft fights in the sky during World War II (1939–1945). One of his most famous planes was a bright-red Fokker **triplane** (below), which had three pairs of wings, one above the other. It earned the deadly Richthofen the nickname "The Red Baron."

GRAF ZEPPELIN

The Graf Zeppelin was a massive airship measuring 776 feet (236.5 meters) long—that's longer than 23 buses in a row. It first flew in 1928. It was also the first airship that could fly around the world. The Zeppelin was built around a long, thin, tube-shaped frame with big bags containing hydrogen gas inside. The crew and passengers were in a gondola below. Passengers traveled in luxury. There was a kitchen, lounge, and dining room and even comfortable cabins to sleep in.

GONDOLA

The Graf Zeppelin usually cruised at 72 miles (166 kilometers) per hour, 650 feet (198 meters) above ground, but could rise as high as 6,000 feet (1,830 meters) when it needed to cross mountain ranges!

How it works

Hydrogen is lighter than air, so the bags of hydrogen gas provided lift. Adjusting the amount of gas and weight of the ship allowed pilots to control how high the Zeppelin floated. To travel forward, the Zeppelin was driven by propellers powered by engines stored in the gondola. The crew used hinged flaps or rudders to steer the airship.

HINDENBURG DISASTER

At 804 feet (245 meters) long and with four engines, the *Hindenburg* was a giant airship. It took its first flight in 1936, carrying passengers between Germany and the United States. However, in 1937, the **flammable** hydrogen gas inside exploded as it was landing, killing many of the people on board. Amazingly, most crew and passengers survived by jumping from the gondola as the *Hindenburg* touched the ground.

It took just over 30 seconds from when the crew spotted the first flame until the whole back of the airship caught fire.

CHINA CLIPPER

Airships were able to carry lots of passengers for long distances, but after the *Hindenburg* disaster, few people trusted them. "Flying boats" became the next big thing. Flying boats were designed in the early 1930s when the airline Pan Am wanted to start airline services from the United States to Asia across the Pacific Ocean. The problem was that there were few airports along the way. The solution: build planes that could land on water!

The China Clipper was huge. It measured 130 feet (40 meters) from wingtip to wingtip, about 90 feet (27 meters) from nose to tail, and had room for up to 32 passengers. It had four engines and could travel at up to 130 miles (209 kilometers) per hour.

The first flying boat

Pan Am asked major aircraft companies to come up with designs for flying boats. The first design was the Sikorsky S-40, but it was too small and could not fly far enough. The second design, the Martin "China Clipper," went into operation in 1935. Its first flight across the Pacific from San Francisco to Manila took six days, and it carried 58 mailbags containing 110,865 specially stamped letters. It landed by the islands of Hawaii, Midway Island, Wake Island, and Guam along the way.

This China Clipper is landing on the ocean. Flying boats were the top design solution to trans-ocean flight up to World War II.

The end of the Clippers

The age of passenger flying boats came to an end during World War II because the Pacific Ocean became a war zone. Designers turned their attention to building and improving war aircraft instead.

Design constraint

An important design constraint on the flying boats was that they had to be watertight and balance on sometimes choppy water. The planes had boat-shaped fuselages with a double skin to make sure no water could get in. They had flotation devices on the wings so that they would not sink.

SPITFIRE

World War II provided new opportunities for aircraft designers. Air forces needed a variety of aircraft, including fast fighter airplanes to attack and defend against enemy airplanes. The iconic fighter of the era was the Spitfire of 1936.

The name "Spitfire" was taken from an old English word meaning someone of strong or fiery character.

New form

In the 1930s, most airplanes were biplanes, but the Spitfire had a new design. It had one pair of large, almost oval wings that helped the airplane to maneuver easily. The wings were deep enough for the wheels to fold into during flight, to reduce drag. The Spitfire was also **aerodynamic** because of its curved body with an enclosed cockpit for the pilot.

Due to its good design, the Spitfire remained the major fighter aircraft used by British forces until 1954.

Air power

The Spitfire used a newly developed Rolls Royce Merlin engine to supply the thrust. The engine gave the Spitfire a maximum speed of 364 miles (585 kilometers) per hour! The wings hid eight powerful machine guns for firepower. Later, these were replaced by four automatic cannons.

High flier

The Spitfire was highly successful in World War II. Pilots loved it because it was easy to handle and it was easily adapted. For example, some Spitfires carried bombs and others took photos of enemy forces. They could fly at **altitudes** of over 6 miles (10 kilometers) high, out of reach of many other enemy planes. **Allied forces** used Spitfires to win the Battle of Britain. The battle was a major air fight that helped changed the course of World War II in favor of the Allies.

WORLD OF DESIGN

Design specification

A **design specification** is a list of the functions, look, materials, costs, and other requirements for a new object, vehicle, or building. The Spitfire's **specification** included high speed and ability to carry machine guns.

Reginald Mitchell

Reginald Mitchell became interested in aircraft in school, where he designed and flew model airplanes. At age 16, he started as an apprentice at a locomotive engineering company. After five years of study, he successfully applied for a job at Supermarine.

Seaplane designer

Mitchell soon became chief engineer and designer at Supermarine. He created many famous seaplanes, including a military flying boat called the Southampton in 1925. It was used until 1936. He was also responsible for many marine speed planes developed to win races and beat speed records. For example, the famous S6B of 1931 won the prestigious Schneider Trophy race and was the fastest airplane in the world for several years, at 407 miles (655 kilometers) per hour.

Spitfire factories

Spitfires were made by Supermarine in its factory in southern England. The UK government wanted so many Spitfires that the company set up a second factory, also in England. After the first factory was bombed and destroyed, planes were built at several smaller factories. These were set up in garages, bus depots, and laundries—places that enemy bombers would not target!

Spitfire success

Mitchell used his experience of building fast aircraft to develop the Spitfire between 1934 and 1936. Over 22,000 Spitfires were built and used worldwide. Sadly, Mitchell never shared in his design's success because he died in 1937, two years before the start of World War II.

Spitfires were put together in large numbers by skilled workers. Each worker was responsible for a particular part or section of the plane.

FLYING FORTRESS

FAST FACTS

Type of aircraft: Bomber
Produced by: Boeing
First flown in: 1936

The Spitfire and other fighter planes were small and able to move quickly, but in World War II, air forces needed large planes to carry and drop bombs, too. The Boeing B-17 is one of the most famous. These U.S. bombers got the name Flying Fortress because they were heavily armed and could stay in the air even when they had been badly damaged. Some even managed to get back to base with large chunks of fuselage shot off!

Over 12,000 Flying Fortresses were made. They flew in every World War II combat zone and dropped many bombs during the war.

High flyer

The Flying Fortress was an all-metal **monoplane** with four engines. It could fly at high altitudes, up to about 35,000 feet (10,670 meters), which took it out of reach of weapons shooting from the ground. It was the first Boeing airplane to have a huge tail, which improved control and kept it steady when bombing from high in the air. It had several turrets with machine guns. The plane could fly for more than eight hours and up to 2,000 miles (3,200 kilometers), to reach targets such as weapons factories deep behind enemy lines. Some could carry as much as 4.5 tons of bombs.

SUPERFORTRESS

The Flying Fortress's big brother, the B-29 Superfortress, could fly farther and carry a heavier load of bombs. It also had new features such as machine guns that fired by remote control. On August 6, 1945, the infamous B-29 *Enola Gay* dropped the world's first atomic bomb on Hiroshima, Japan.

This is the view from the front turret. Crew members defended the plane from attack using powerful machine guns.

MESSERSCHMITT ME 262

FAST FACTS

Type of aircraft: Jet-powered fighter plane
Produced by: Messerschmitt
First flown in: 1942 (with jet engine)

Toward the end of World War II, a totally new kind of aircraft entered the battle zone. This plane had no propeller, but it could race through the air at more than 500 miles (800 kilometers) per hour. The Messerschmitt Me 262 was developed in 1942, and it was the first fighter plane with a **jet engine**. These create thrust by shooting out jets of hot gases!

HOW JET ENGINES WORK

1. A jet engine sucks air into the front part of the engine.
2. A compressor squeezes the air into a combustion chamber.
3. In the combustion chamber, fuel is added and burned to create hot gases.
4. The hot gases are blasted out of a nozzle, creating the thrust force that pushes the aircraft forward.

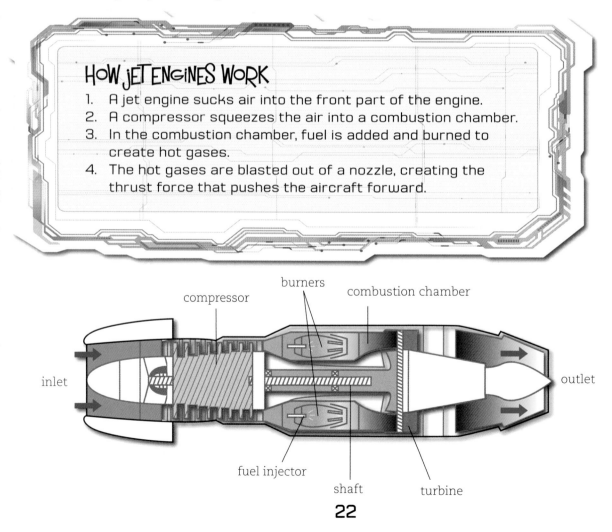

inlet

compressor

burners

combustion chamber

outlet

fuel injector

shaft

turbine

War changer?

The Messerschmitt Me 262 could fly about 100 miles (161 kilometers) per hour faster than other fighter planes. It had powerful cannons and it was highly acrobatic in the air. However, the materials needed to make its high-temperature engine were scarce, so Messerschmitts were not produced until 1944. This was too late for them to make a difference in the war's outcome. By then, Allied forces were already moving into German-controlled regions and getting closer to invading Germany itself.

JET PIONEER

British engineer Frank Whittle had designed the very first jet engine by 1930, but he had difficulties getting the engine to work properly. German engineers working on a jet engine at the same time achieved the first jet-powered flight in 1939, with the Heinkel He 178.

The German Messerschmitt Me 262 was the only jet fighter plane in combat service during World War II. It was first used in 1944.

SIKORSKY S-55

FAST FACTS

Type of aircraft: Utility helicopter
Produced by: Sikorsky
First flown in: 1949

FIRST HELICOPTERS

Igor Sikorsky had experimented with model flying machines from an early age. At 12 years old, he made a small rubber-powered helicopter that could rise into the air! He designed and made many airplanes, including flying boats, and in 1939, his first helicopter, the VS-300, lifted off the ground, with Sikorsky at the controls. In 1941, an improved version made a record flight of 1 hour, 32.4 seconds.

In 1949, another new type of aircraft appeared: the Sikorsky S-55 helicopter. Designers had known about the benefits of helicopters for a while. Unlike planes, helicopters could take off and land from a small space and hover in one spot. However, the first models were small and not very practical. The S-55 was the first really successful helicopter design.

An iconic design

Like other helicopters, the S-55 uses blades shaped like narrow wings to create lift. These are called **rotors**. As they spin, the rotors create a downward push against the air. This makes the helicopter rise up. The S-55 was widely used from the start. It helped the armed forces to save around 10,000 wounded soldiers in the Korean War (1950–1953) by airlifting them from the battlefield to get medical treatment. It was also used for rescues at sea.

STOP SPINNING

Many helicopters have rotors at the back. These give a sideways push to stop a helicopter fuselage from twisting around as the main rotor spins. Some stop spinning in other ways. For example, the giant Chinook helicopter (see photograph below) has two rotors on top that spin in opposite directions, to balance each other out.

HARRIER JUMP JET

While helicopters can go straight up and down, most aircraft need to drive along a runway to gain enough speed before taking off. The Harrier jump jet is different. This iconic airplane can vertically take off and land (known as "VTOL"). It has four nozzles that direct the jet engine thrust downward in order to make the jet fly straight up.

FLYING BEDSTEAD

The Harrier was based on an earlier attempt to make a VTOL craft called the "Flying bedstead," also known as the Rolls-Royce Thrust Measuring Rig. It consisted of a metal frame with four legs and a seat for the pilot in the middle. It had two jet engines pointing in opposite directions. Unfortunately, it crashed and killed the pilot testing it.

The Hawker Harrier jet combines the best aspects of a helicopter with those of a fighter jet.

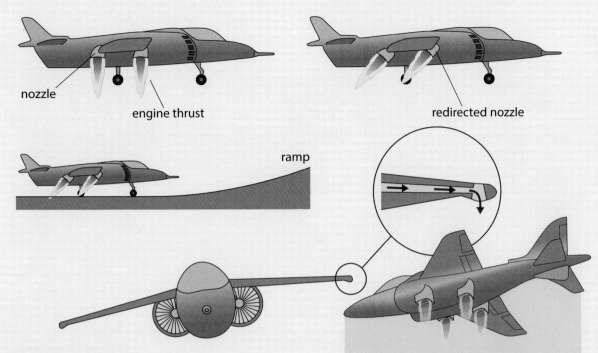

nozzle

engine thrust

redirected nozzle

ramp

Helpful Harrier

The Hawker Harrier was first designed in 1957 by British engineer Sidney Camm. It was designed to fly from battle zones and small **aircraft carriers** and to help soldiers on the ground. It took a long time to develop into a fully working model, so it didn't fly until 1966. It could carry several types of weapons, including missiles, rockets, and bombs. It was mainly used to protect naval ships and the soldiers working from them.

The Harrier has one jet engine and four main nozzles that direct the jet engine thrust downward for vertical lift. In the air, the nozzles are redirected so that the plane moves forward. Using a ramp for takeoff saves fuel, as forward motion provides some lift. Extra small nozzles in the wing help the plane to move when hovering.

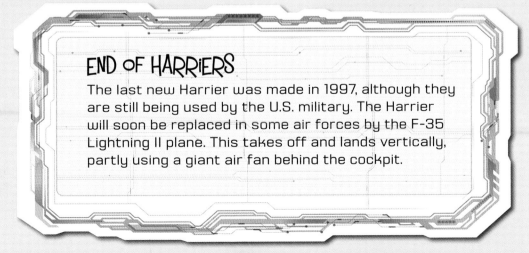

END OF HARRIERS

The last new Harrier was made in 1997, although they are still being used by the U.S. military. The Harrier will soon be replaced in some air forces by the F-35 Lightning II plane. This takes off and lands vertically, partly using a giant air fan behind the cockpit.

Learjet

FAST FACTS

Date: 1963
Designer: William Powell Lear
Type of aircraft: private jet
Wingspan: 35 feet, 7 inches (10.8 meters) wingspan
Special features: tapering body, clamshell doors, external twin jet engines
Top speed: 560 miles (903 kilometers) per hour
Did you know? Lear left school early and invented the first car radio in the 1920s!

William Powell "Bill" Lear invented the car radio and the eight-track tape player before he became an aircraft designer. He used the money he made from these inventions for his jet project.

With the world wars long over and an increase in wealth, aircraft designers began designing more pleasure and business airplanes than military craft. The Learjet was the first and most famous private jet.

Concept

William P. Lear was a millionaire inventor who, in the late 1950s, decided to create a reasonably priced, speedy private jet. He believed it would be in demand from people, such as business executives, who wanted to travel places fast without waiting for scheduled airline flights. Back then, the only alternatives were converted, slow, expensive military aircraft.

Design

Lear hired engineers to help him design a plane based on a Swiss-built fighter-bomber, the P-16. The major design specification was for a small aircraft that could cruise as fast as **airliners** (over 500 miles/800 kilometers per hour). The engineers reduced the weight of the plane to help it go faster. They moved the engines outside the body to make room for four passengers and tapered the fuselage to reduce drag. New design features included a wraparound windshield and an outward-opening "clamshell" door.

Development in the air

Lear spent millions of dollars of his own money developing a working prototype of the Learjet. It was unusual to go straight to a flying aircraft rather than making smaller models to test. But Lear's team used data and observations of many test flights in the air to perfect their design.

Cheap development

Today, it can cost almost $1 billion over 10 years to develop a new jet aircraft from **design concept** to production. Lear made this happen in just over 1 year for just $12 million.

Flight success

The prototype, called the Learjet 23, first flew in October 1963. The test pilots were amazed by its performance and ease of handling. It accelerated and flew as fast as any military plane they had flown. By 1964, the aircraft had been approved for safety and sale. Early buyers who could afford the price—over $500,000—included large corporations and also rich celebrities such as the singer Frank Sinatra.

Record breaker

In 1965, the Learjet 23 set several records. These included flying from Los Angeles to New York and back in less than 11 hours, including refueling stops. It also broke a record by climbing from the ground to 40,000 feet (12,192 meters) in seven minutes!

The original Learjets were small but luxurious inside.

Adjusting design

However, the Learjet 23 was very powerful, and many crashed. Lear made changes to the design, including an engine that handled better at lower speeds in the Lear 24. Later models could fly farther with more passengers, but all are based on the original groundbreaking design. Lear had to sell his company, but the Learjet name has continued into the 21st century.

The Learjet was a new category of aircraft— the private jet.

Lucky crash

In 1964, disaster struck on a test flight of the Lear 23 prototype when it crashed and burst into flames. Fortunately, the pilots escaped. Lear had spent most of his money on testing by then. But, luckily, he was paid accident insurance money. He used this money to help get the Learjet approved by the authorities.

JUMBO JET

FAST FACTS

Type of aircraft: Long-range jet airliner
Produced by: Boeing Commercial Aircraft
First flown in: 1969

In 1963, the engineering team at Boeing started to plan a new, big aircraft. They anticipated the demand for cheaper flights and increased air transportation of **freight**. The Boeing 747, or jumbo jet, was the product of this planning.

Jumbo jets are still in use today. To date, the global fleet of around 1,500 jumbo jets has carried around 5.6 billion passengers.

JUMBO TRAINING

The jumbo jet has a wing area larger than a basketball court and a tail taller than a six-story building. Pilots needed special training to handle these enormous planes. For example, Waddell's Wagon was a truck with three-story-high stilts and a 747 cockpit on top. Pilots learned to maneuver the jumbo jet by directing the truck driver below.

Design for the future

Designers led by Joe Sutter came up with an **innovative** wide-bodied airplane in which three rows of passengers could sit side by side. It would be able to hold 350 or more passengers. Designers put the heavy, massive engines under the wings rather than near the tail, to balance the great weight. The cockpit and passenger lounge were on a hump on top of the airplane. This made it possible to convert jumbo jets to freight planes, by fitting a hinged nose cone for easy loading.

In the late 1960s, most airliners had capacities of around 150 passengers. The jumbo jet carried over twice this number, due to its wide body.

Birth of the legend

News about the new airplane spread. Soon, the airline Pan Am had ordered 25. By 1966, Boeing had built a production plant to make the 747, and the first working prototype flew in 1969. The jumbo jet rapidly became the large airliner of choice for global airlines soon after its first commercial service in 1970.

Designer in Focus

Joe Sutter

Joe Sutter grew up in Seattle, Washington, under the flight path of passing airplanes from a nearby airport. He built and designed model airplanes from a young age. This interest developed, and he went on to study aeronautical engineering at the University of Washington. Sutter paid for his tuition using earnings from a paper route and also part-time work in the Seattle-based Boeing factory.

Joe Sutter visited one of the latest jumbo jet versions, the 747-8, in 2012.

WORLD OF DESIGN

Aeronautical engineer

Aeronautical engineers research, design, develop, maintain, and test the performance, safety, and efficiency of flying machines. Sutter used science and technology to design and engineer the jumbo jet.

Rise at Boeing

Sutter fought in the U.S. Navy in World War II and then studied at the Navy's aviation engineering school. Soon he joined Boeing so he could be near home. Sutter quickly got a reputation as an excellent and practical designer of aerodynamic aircraft. By the mid-1960s, he was in charge of a team of around 4,000 people often called "The Incredibles." They were working on the enormous and innovative 747 project.

Lifetime work

For 10 years, Sutter led the program of improving and adapting the plane for freight and other purposes. He was then made Boeing's chief of engineering, a role he kept until he retired. However, he still takes part in Boeing meetings today.

You can see many jumbo jets in use at airports today.

CONCORDE

The same year that the jumbo jet first flew also saw the appearance of Concorde. Many people in the airline industry believed that the future was **supersonic** planes such as Concorde. Supersonic means flying faster than the speed of sound, which is 768 miles (1,235 kilometers) per hour. Passengers could now reach their destinations faster than ever before.

STEALING IDEAS

In 1968, the Russian supersonic airliner Tupolev Tu-144 had its first flight. Its design was remarkably similar to Concorde because spies had stolen Concorde designs and data and smuggled them to Russia!

Its big wings meant Concorde had to take off and land at a steep angle. That's why designers made a bending nose— so the pilots could see the runway!

Designed for speed

Concorde was unmistakable. Its body was shaped like a pointed rocket and it had massive triangular wings—a bit like an enormous paper airplane! The **streamlined** shape and swept-back wings reduced the extra drag at high speeds. Concorde had the most powerful jet engines available. They produced extra thrust by using hot exhaust gases to burn extra fuel.

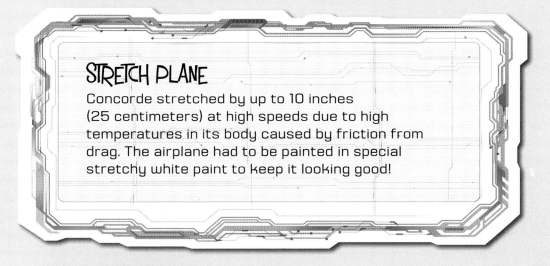

STRETCH PLANE

Concorde stretched by up to 10 inches (25 centimeters) at high speeds due to high temperatures in its body caused by friction from drag. The airplane had to be painted in special stretchy white paint to keep it looking good!

Record breaker

Concorde could fly at more than twice the speed of sound at much greater heights than normal airliners. It broke many flight records, including London to New York in less than three hours in 1996! This was a third of the time taken by normal airliners. Flying by Concorde was in demand, especially among business travelers.

A tragic end

Concorde's reputation for safety was seriously affected by a tragedy at Charles de Gaulle Airport in Paris, in 2000. One of an Air France Concorde's four engines caught fire soon after takeoff, and the plane crashed and exploded, killing 113 people. Concordes were already not very profitable aircraft because of the high cost of building and maintaining the unique supersonic technology. This meant that ticket prices were very high. After the crash and because of the high price, this iconic plane stopped flying in 2003, and supersonic passenger flight was over.

SPACE SHUTTLE ORBITER

FAST FACTS

Type of aircraft: Space plane
Produced by: Rockwell International
First flown in: 1981

In 1981, an astonishing new aircraft blasted off into space: the space shuttle orbiter. After spending some days in space, astronauts could fly the orbiter home. They could repeat this trip time and again.

A cheaper solution

Before the orbiter, all astronauts and space vehicles had been carried inside rockets whose parts had been discarded during flight. This was very expensive and wasteful. The new orbiter changed all that. The shuttle needed booster rockets to carry it upward. These dropped away from the orbiter once it was near space and parachuted back to Earth for re-use. Only the enormous fuel tank that was needed to get the orbiter into space became a throwaway part once it was empty.

Orbiters flew at over 200 miles (320 kilometers) above Earth as spacecraft before becoming aircraft once more on the journey back to our planet.

Orbiter design

The orbiter was 122 feet, 2 inches (37.24 meters) long. That's longer than three school buses. It had a cockpit and living quarters at the front and big opening doors on top with space to transport things. Orbiters were used to launch satellites and parts for building space stations where astronauts lived for long periods. The orbiter underside was covered with black tiles that could absorb heat. Without these, the vehicle may have been damaged upon flying into Earth's **atmosphere** from space. The drag caused by flying at around 17,000 miles (27,000 kilometers) per hour into Earth's air created temperatures of 3,002 degrees Fahrenheit (1,650 degrees Celsius).

END OF THE SHUTTLES

Six orbiters were built. One never flew in space, but five completed hundreds of successful missions. However, the space shuttle program came to an end in 2011. This was partly because of two disasters when orbiters blew up. *Challenger* blew up shortly after takeoff. *Colombia* blew up on the journey home. It was also because by then there were cheaper ways to transport things into space.

The orbiter *Atlantic* used a parachute and a flap on its tail to slow the shuttle down quickly after touchdown.

B-2 STEALTH BOMBER

FAST FACTS

Type of aircraft: Bomber
Produced by: Northrop Corporation
First flown in: 1989

Back on Earth, the race to improve military bombers continued. The trouble was that aircraft are mostly visible to enemies on the ground using **radar**. Enemies also had better and better weapons to shoot them down. So, designers invented the B-2, or stealth bomber.

Designed not to be seen

The stealth bomber looks like a giant jagged boomerang. Its outline was designed using computers that calculated which shapes best confuse radar systems. The B-2 is also coated in paints and made of materials that either absorb or deflect the radio waves used in radar systems. It looks like a flying sparrow to a radar system! The stealth bomber has machines to cool any hot gases coming from the jet engines, so it cannot be detected by the heat it releases, either.

The B-2 shape is unlike the standard fuselage (with wings and tail sticking out) that is found on most airplanes.

This diagram shows the measurements of the stealth bomber. Its unusual shape helps it stay hidden when flying.

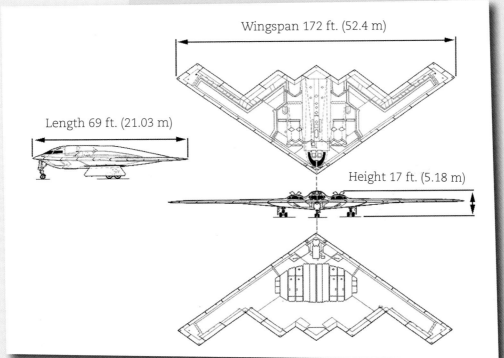

Wingspan 172 ft. (52.4 m)

Length 69 ft. (21.03 m)

Height 17 ft. (5.18 m)

HOW RADAR WORKS

Radar is a system in which a machine sends out a beam of radio waves and detects any that bounce back after hitting an object. Waves bounce back more off hard materials such as metal and less off softer plastics. People can use radar to figure out not only where aircraft are, but also how fast they are moving and where they are heading.

Long-range bombing

The B-2 can fly bombing missions of 6,800 miles (11,000 kilometers) without refueling. It has been used in many conflicts around the world. It has good **fuel economy** because the 172-feet- (52-meter-) wide wing produces so much lift. However, the B-2 uses costly modern technology and is expensive to maintain. That is why only 20 of these airplanes, which cost over $2 billion each, have ever been made.

THE FUTURE OF AIRCRAFT DESIGN

This book has introduced just a few of the most iconic aircraft from the past and present. We have seen how designers made better performing vehicles for particular purposes. What will aircraft be like in the future?

Energy-saving designs

Aircraft makers of the future will **commission** aircraft that fly using less fuel. This constraint will be very important because supplies of fuel are dwindling across the globe. Fuel use is also contributing to **global warming** and air pollution. Many future airliners will also use lightweight materials for lower weight. They will use new aerodynamic shapes such as long, thin wings attached to the tail, or "flying wing" styles similar to the stealth bomber. Some will have **hybrid engines** that use fuel mostly for takeoff and will cruise using electric motors. Others may be supersonic like Concorde, but then may cruise in space. Noise is not a problem in space and there is no air to cause drag.

In 2003, there was the first flight of a totally solar-powered electric airplane called Helios. The flight proved that fuel-free powered flight was possible.

Pilotless aircraft

One way to cut flight costs and increase human safety is to use **drones** or robot aircraft. In 1995, the first modern drone was put into operation by the U.S. military. It tracked enemy movements using onboard cameras and other equipment. Soon drones were being used to fire missiles on enemies. Today, there are tens of thousands of drones worldwide, not just for military uses. Some are used to spot when crops are ready to pick, while others deliver goods in busy cities. Scientists use drones to study dangerous volcanoes.

WORLD OF DESIGN

Commission

A design commission is a request from an individual, company, or even government to design something.

This pilot of a drone sits in an office to fly his aircraft using radio-controlled signals from a computer. Could there be more pilotless robot aircraft in the future?

TIMELINE

1783 Montgolfier brothers make the first human flight in a hot-air balloon

1853 George Cayley makes the world's first glider that can carry a person

1890 In France, Clement Ader claims he has flown his steam-powered airplane, but there is no proof

1903 Wright *Flyer I* makes the first powered flight

1909 Bleriot makes the first crossing of the English Channel in an airplane

1916 Sopwith Camel is invented. It went on to shoot down more enemy fighters than any other aircraft in World War I.

1927 Charles Lindbergh makes the first solo flight across the Atlantic

1928 Graf Zeppelin invents the first airship to fly around the world

1930 Frank Whittle invents the jet engine

1935 Martin "China Clipper" flying boat is invented and makes the first flight across the Pacific Ocean

1936 Spitfire fighter plane is invented for use in World War II

1941 B-17 Flying Fortress bomber is first used by Allied air forces

1942 Messerschmitt Me 262 is the first operational jet fighter plane

1947 Chuck Yeager makes the first supersonic flight

1949 Sikorsky S-55 is invented and becomes the world's first successful helicopter

1957 Harrier jump jet is invented— the world's first airplane that can take off and land vertically

1963 Learjet is the first affordable but high-performance private jet

1969 Boeing 747, or the jumbo jet, first flies and soon becomes the world's most popular large airliner

1969 Concorde supersonic airliner is invented

1981 The space shuttle orbiter aircraft travels to space and back

1988 The biggest ever aircraft, An-225, is invented. It can lift 280 tons.

1989 B-2 stealth bomber is flown

1995 The first military drone is used

2010 Solar Impulse flies for 24 hours nonstop using just solar power

2013 Boeing tests a hypersonic airplane that can fly at over five times the speed of sound

GLOSSARY

aerodynamic describes how well something moves through the air

aircraft carrier military ship with a landing strip for aircraft

airfoil structure with curved surfaces to provide maximum lift and minimum drag when moving through the air

airliner large airplane used to carry many passengers

airship aircraft that produces lift using trapped gasses that are lighter than air and that is moved along using propellers

Allied forces countries that fought together against Germany in World War I and World War II

altitude height above Earth's surface at sea level

atmosphere band of gases surrounding Earth that ends when space begins

biplane airplane with two pairs of wings

cockpit compartment where a pilot and sometimes other members of a flight crew sit and operate an aircraft

commission assign someone to create or produce something, such as a new car

design concept idea, invention, or plan

design specification wish list of the features, shape, and capabilities an object will ideally have

drag another word for "air resistance," a force that pushes against a moving object, like air pushing against an airplane's wing

drone unmanned robot aircraft

engineer person who designs and builds machines, structures, or engines using scientific methods

flammable catches fire easily

freight goods transported in bulk by air, sea, or road

fuel economy describes how far a vehicle can travel on a certain amount of fuel

fuselage main part of an airplane to which wings and a tail are attached

glider type of aircraft that stays airborne with no engine or motor

global warming gradual rise in Earth's average temperature caused by gases in the atmosphere trapping the Sun's heat

gravity force pulling objects toward Earth

hybrid engine engine that combines a gasoline engine with another type of engine, such as an electric motor

innovative describes a new, original idea or way of doing something

jet engine type of engine that provides thrust forward when hot gases flow fast backward

monoplane airplane with one pair of wings

propeller angled blades that create a push when they spin fast

prototype first version of a design, which is then copied and improved upon

radar system for finding distant objects by sending out radio waves and detecting their echoes

rotor moving blades on helicopters that produce thrust (*see* propeller)

specification detailed description of how a design or something else should be done

streamlined shaped to reduce air resistance and move through the air easily and quickly

supersonic faster than the speed of sound

thrust force usually produced by an engine to push an aircraft forward

triplane airplane with three pairs of wings

wind tunnel space used to test the flow of air past objects such as aircraft

FIND OUT MORE

Books

Brook, Henry. *Fighter Planes.* Tulsa, OK.: EDC, 2012.

Grant, Reg. *Flight: The Trials and Triumphs of Air Pioneers.* New York: Dorling Kindersley, 2003.

LaPadula, Tom. *Learn to Draw Planes, Choppers and Watercraft.* Irvine, CA.: Walter Foster, 2013.

Tudor, Andy. *200 Paper Planes to Fold and Fly.* Tulsa, OK.: EDC, 2013.

Wesselhoeft, Conrad. *Dirt Bikes, Drones, and Other Ways to Fly.* Boston: Houghton Mifflin Harcourt, 2015.

Internet Sites

Facthound offers a safe, fun way to find Internet sites related to this book. All of the sites on Facthound have been researched by our staff.

Here's all you do:

Visit www.facthound.com

Type in this code: 9781484626160

Ideas for research

If you would like to be an aerospace engineer one day, then find out what skills you might need to develop and which colleges offer programs in aerospace engineering. Read interviews with aircraft designers to learn about what the work is like.

Places to visit

The Exploratorium
Pier 15 (Embarcadero at Green Street)
San Francisco, California 94111
Tel: (415) 528-4444
E-mail: visit@exploratorium.edu
Web site: www.exploratorium.edu

Learn more about the science behind flight at this amazing interactive science museum.

The Museum of Flight
9404 E. Marginal Way South
Seattle, Washington 98108
Tel: (206) 764-5700
E-mail: info@museumofflight.org
Web site: www.museumofflight.org

At this museum, you can see real aircraft, as well as many exhibits showcasing inventions and achievements throughout the history of human flight.

Smithsonian National Air and Space Museum
600 Independence Avenue Southwest
Washington, D.C. 20560
Tel: (202) 633-2214
E-mail: nasmweb@si.edu
Web site: airandspace.si.edu

This museum has the largest collection of aircraft and spacecraft in the world, including examples of the Wright Brothers' Flyer, planes from World War II, and examples up to the present day, plus many amazing interactive exhibits.

INDEX